Who's in a Family?

Robert Skutch

Illustrations by Laura Nienhaus

Tricycle Press
Berkeley, California

TRICYCLE PRESS
P.O. Box 7123
Berkeley, California 94707

Library of Congress Cataloging-in-Publication Data
Skutch, Robert.
Who's in a family? / Robert Skutch :
illustrations by Laura Nienhaus.
p.   cm.
"Age level: 3 to 6"—CIP data sheet.
ISBN 1-883672-13-9
1. Family—Juvenile literature. 2. Familial behavior—Juvenile literature.
[1. Family. 2. Family life.]   I. Nienhaus, Laura, ill.   II. Title.
HQ734.S665 1994
306.85—dc20   94-29635
                                         CIP
                                          AC

First Tricycle Press printing, 1995
Manufactured in Singapore
2 3 4 5 6 — 98 97 96 95

This book is dedicated to
the loving family of
Lindsay, Gail, Clay, and Will.

A family can be made up
in many different ways.

My Family

Families are made up of people,

and animals
have families, too.

In Carlos' family, Carlos' papá
helps him with his homework,
and his mamá reads to
his little sisters,
Teresa and
Linda.

Katie is an only child. When Katie's family goes camping, she sometimes gets to take along her friend, Amy.

Amina and Geitha live with their father. They love
it when he puts on a puppet show for them.

Lots of children live in families with their mothers.
Janet plays ball with Josh and Ryan until their mom,
Catherine, comes home.

That's like the chimpanzee family. Mama chimp raises the babies by herself, with the help of any older children she may have.

Laura and Kyle live with their mom, Joyce, her partner, Emily, and a poodle named Daisy. It takes all four of them to give Daisy her bath.

In Kevin's family, Grandmother Kyoko takes care of Kevin and his brother, Jeffrey, while their mother is at work. They like their grandmother to help them put together jigsaw puzzles.

In elephant families, the oldest female elephant is in full charge of a family made up of only mothers, aunts, teenagers, and babies.

Male elephants live together
in their own family.

Aunt Amanda and Uncle Stan don't have
any children at all, but they're still a family.
They say Mouser and Fred are their "babies."

Ricky has two families. Most of the time, he lives with his mom. But when Ricky visits his dad, he has a baby sister to play with.

In lion families there is only one father,
but lots of babies and several mothers
to take care of them and get them food.

Robin's family is made up of her dad, Clifford, her dad's partner, Henry, and Robin's cat, Sassy. Clifford and Henry take turns making dinner for their family.

Families can look different
from each other...

...and even in the same family, family members can look different from one another.

In Eric's family, his daddy has light skin and his mommy has dark skin. That's why the color of Eric's skin is in-between.

And Karen doesn't look like her dad or her mom, but she has her grandpa's smile.

And two of
Cleo's puppies
are all white,
one is brown,
and two
have spots.

Who's in a
family?

The people who
love you the most!

Just like in
your family.

Here's a place for you to
draw a picture of your family.